IT ALL BEGINS

Of course we know that the newest addition to our family is amazing, but finding the time and energy to record for posterity can be challenging. Through the new smells, messy feedings, foggy nights, and overwhelming sense of awe, let **Pleased to Meet You!** be your guide. You'll find prompts to document all the little details, along with the big milestones. For each blissful moment of parenthood, there are a handful of unglorified times that will be just as much fun to look back on.

Remember to pause, take note, and reflect on all that happens in this unbelievable year. The result will be a refreshing account of the steps from baby to toddler, and a heartwarming portrait of your growing family.

—Kate Pocrass

NAME

PASTE
PHOTO
HERE

BIRTHDAY

TIME OF BIRTH

WEIGHING IN AT

LENGTH

YOU'VE ARRIVED

WHERE I WAS WHEN
MY WATER BROKE:

KEPT MY COOL
OR FREAKED OUT:

ALL AS EXPECTED
OR CHANGE IN PLANS:

SOME NOTES:

PURE BLISS — SHORT-LIVED & WELL WORTH IT — EASIER THAN EXPECTED — YIKES, THAT HURT

LABOR PAIN-O-METER

WHERE YOU WERE BORN: ....

DOCTOR OR MIDWIFE: ....

NURSE OR DOULA: ....

WHO CUT THE CORD: ....

WHO WAS BESIDE MOM: ....

WANT TO REMEMBER: ....

....

....

....

....

....

....

....

....

....

....

....

....

....

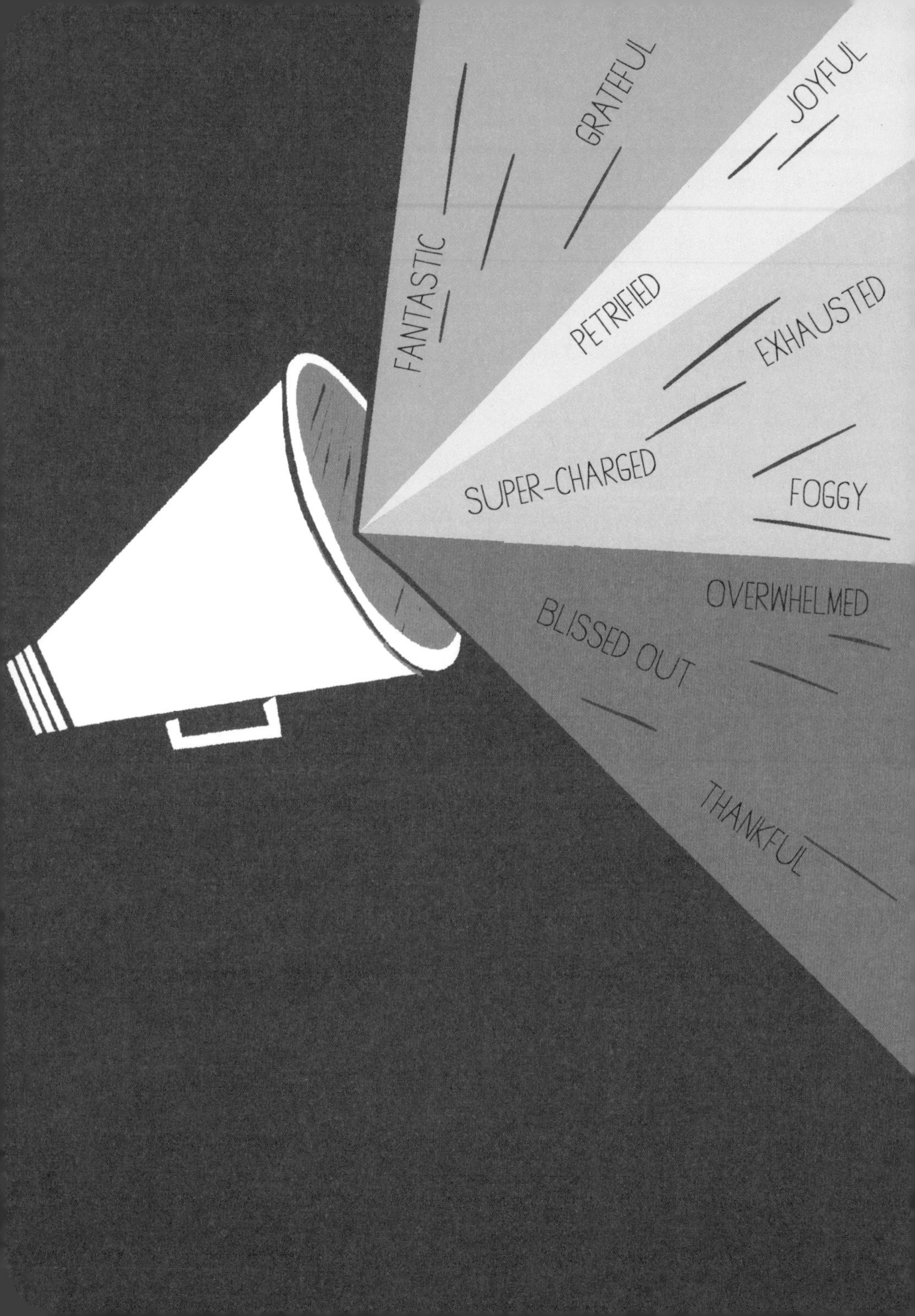
FANTASTIC
GRATEFUL
JOYFUL
PETRIFIED
EXHAUSTED
SUPER-CHARGED
FOGGY
OVERWHELMED
BLISSED OUT
THANKFUL

SOME THOUGHTS ABOUT PARENTHOOD

NEW
MOON

WAXING
CRESCENT

FIRST
QUARTER

WAXING
GIBBOUS

FULL MOON

WANING
GIBBOUS

LAST
QUARTER

WANING
CRESCENT

NEW
MOON

TIME OF DAY:

DAY OF THE WEEK:

THE WEATHER WAS:

THE PHASE OF THE MOON WAS:

YOUR ZODIAC SIGN IS:

OTHER MYSTIC THINGS TO NOTE:

VERY IMPORTANT DECISION-MAKING

YOUR NAME

NAME

SPECIAL MEANING

OTHER CONTENDERS

NAME

SPECIAL MEANING

A FEW OF YOUR NICKNAMES

NICKNAME

WHO CALLS YOU THAT

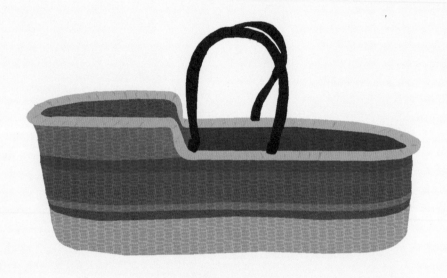

ALL WE NEED IS A REALLY
CUTE BASSINET, RIGHT?

PEOPLE WHO . . .

SENT SOMETHING

KEPT US WELL-FED

ACTED AS A MAKESHIFT
ADVICE HOTLINE

HELD THE CRYING BABY

PEOPLE WHO CAME TO VISIT

FRIENDS & FAMILY WHO LENT A HAND

WHO

HOW THEY HELPED

SO
MUCH
NEW-
NESS

DAILY REMINDERS

ONLINE FORUMS ARE BANNED

DOCTOR KNOWS MORE THAN
RANDOM INTERNET SEARCH

RESIST URGE TO LOOK UP
EVERY SYMPTOM BABY HAS

- ☐ PANTS ARE STILL SNUG

- ☐ MEMORY IS STILL MISSING

- ☐ 1000% IN LOVE WITH BABY

- ☐ STILL CAN'T BELIEVE I HAVE A BABY

- ☐ PETRIFIED OF LOUD NOISES WAKING YOU UP

- ☐ ENJOYING HOW STRANGERS OOGLE OVER HOW CUTE YOU ARE

- ☐ PONDERING HOW SUCH A TINY THING POOPS SO MUCH

- ☐ SLOWLY DECIPHERING YOUR CRIES

- ☐ LOVING HOW BUFF MY ARMS ARE FROM CARRYING YOU 24/7

- ☐ CAN'T SEEM TO REMEMBER TO FEED MYSELF

- ☐ CANNOT COMPREHEND HOW YOU GET OUT OF THAT SWADDLE

- ☐ STARING AT YOU IS CERTAINLY MY NEW FAVORITE PASTIME

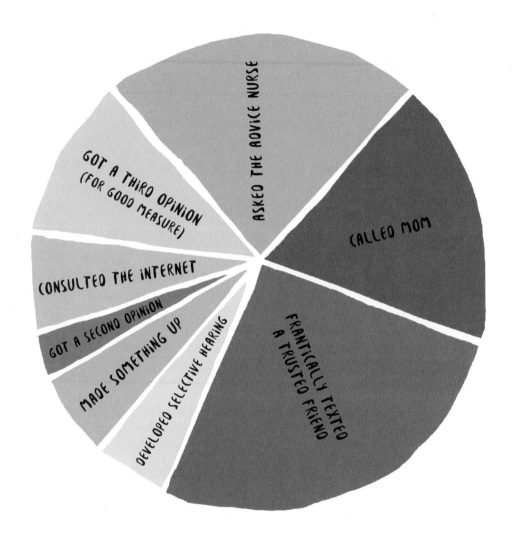

IN MOMENTS OF PARENTAL UNCERTAINTY

TRUSTED ADVICE TAKEN

WHO   WHAT THEY SUGGESTED

....

....

....

....

....

....

....

....

....

FUNNY ADVICE POLITELY DECLINED

WHO   WHAT THEY SUGGESTED

....

....

....

....

....

....

....

....

....

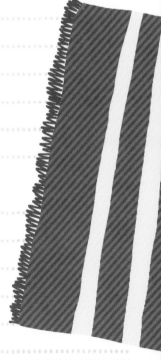

NAPPING WITH YOU
ON A BLANKET
UNDER A SHADY TREE

FRESH BABY
POST-BATH SMELL

DIAPER PAIL SMELL

STALE MILK-SOAKED
BURP CLOTH SMELL

MISSING THE LITTLE THINGS:
- ☐ HAPPY HOUR
- ☐ GOING OUT TO A MOVIE
- ☐ LEAVING THE HOUSE QUICKLY
- ☐ NO-ALARM-CLOCK WEEKENDS

"NEH"
HUNGRY

"EH"
BURP ME

"OWH"
TIRED

"EAIRH"
GAS

WAS THAT AN "EH" I JUST
HEARD, OR A "NEH?"

"HEH"
UNCOMFORTABLE

PARENTING METHODS WE TRIED

- [ ]
- [ ]
- [ ]
- [ ]
- [ ]
- [ ]
- [ ]
- [ ]
- [ ]
- [ ]

PRODUCTS WE COULDN'T LIVE WITHOUT

- [ ]
- [ ]
- [ ]
- [ ]
- [ ]
- [ ]
- [ ]
- [ ]
- [ ]
- [ ]

SPONGE

BUCKET

SINK

HOSE

☐ YOU THINK WATER IS HILARIOUS

☐ YOU THINK WATER IS TERRIFYING

☐ I HAD NO IDEA SOMETHING COULD BE THIS SLIPPERY

☐ WHY CAN'T SOMEONE BOTTLE FRESH-BABY SMELL?

☐ IT SURE IS HARD TO WASH BETWEEN YOUR ROLLS

☐ WHEN DO YOU GRADUATE OUT OF THE SINK?

☐ I THOUGHT THIS SHAMPOO GUARANTEED NO TEARS?

☐ BABY + BUBBLES: COULD NOT GET ANY CUTER

☐ ....

☐ ....

☐ ....

THE WRAP:
- ☐ READ INSTRUCTIONS
- ☐ FOUND ONLINE TUTORIAL
- ☐ 2 HOURS OF POSITIONING
- ☐ CONSULTED MOM FRIEND

HOW LONG IT TAKES TO LEAVE THE HOUSE:

PREFERRED METHOD OF BABY CARRYING:

NEVER LEAVE THE HOUSE WITHOUT:

A GOOD MOMENT OF WANDERING WITH BABY:

SUPERNATURAL
WALL-PENETRATING HEARING

SHOWERING SELF WHILE
ENTERTAINING BABY

MASTERED THE ART OF
ONE-HANDED DEXTERITY

ABILITY TO FIND ALL
MISPLACED PACIFIERS

NOT WAKING THE BABY
YOU'RE HOLDING EVEN THOUGH
YOUR ARM FELL ASLEEP

72ND LOAD THIS WEEK

☐ CRADLE CAP

☐ PROJECTILE VOMIT

☐ HOW MUCH LAUNDRY THERE WOULD BE

☐ NOT TO BUY ANYTHING WITH BUTTONS

☐ THE FIRST MAGICAL GIGGLE

☐ $\frac{1}{3}$ OF THE GADGETS WE BOUGHT ARE USELESS

☐ ....

☐ ....

☐ ....

☐ ....

☐ ....

☐ ....

FOR THE RECORD

THAT WAS THE BEST THING THAT HAS EVER HAPPENED TO ME

YOU FINALLY SLEPT THROUGH THE NIGHT:

HOW MANY MONTHS

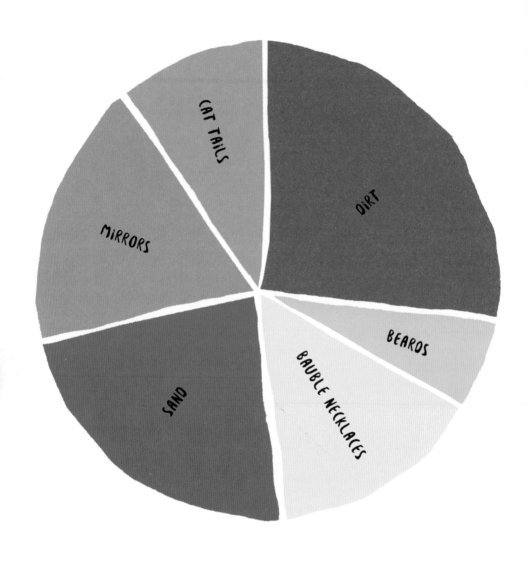

JOY IN THE EXTRA ORDINARY

☐ BEING HELD WAY UP HIGH

☐ SILLY FACES

☐ STUFFED ANIMALS PEEKING OUT FROM BEHIND THE SOFA

☐ WHEN DOGS LICK YOU

☐ ....

☐ ....

☐ ....

☐ ....

☐ ....

☐ ....

☐ ....

☐ ....

LEAF OR RUBBING FROM A MEMORABLE OUTING

EARLY-MORNING WALK IN THE NEIGHBORHOOD:

MUCH-NEEDED NATURE HIKE:

FUN TIME STROLLING IN THE CITY:

VACATION:

LOCAL:

WEEKENDER:

VISIT TO:

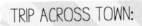

TRIP ACROSS TOWN:

JUST FOR FUN:

FIRST FLIGHT:

FIRST TRAIN:

FIRST BUS:

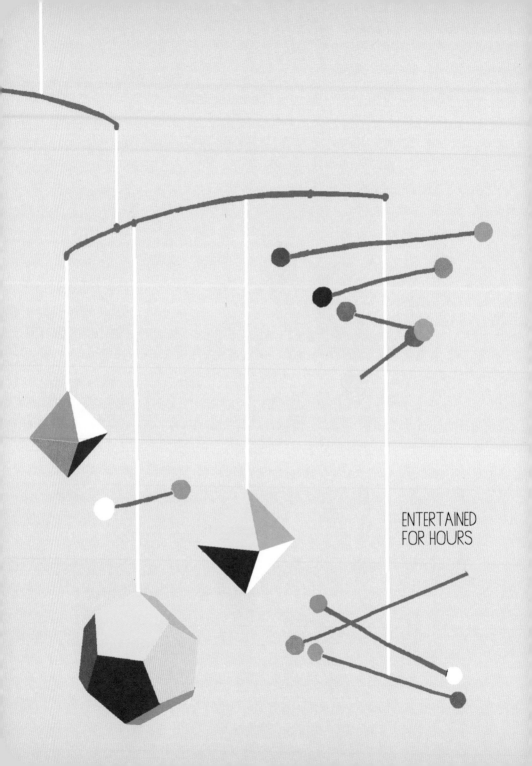

ENTERTAINED
FOR HOURS

YOUR FIRST ROOM LOOKS LIKE:

YOUR FIRST HOUSE IS:

YOUR FIRST NEIGHBORHOOD IS:

YOU

MAMA

GRANDMA

GRANDPA

GRAN

GREAT
GRANDMA

GREAT
GRANDPA

GREAT
GRANDMA

GREAT
GRANDPA

GREAT
GRANDMA

SIBLINGS, UNCLES, AUNTS, COUSINS

....
....
....
....
....

APA

....
....
....
....

GRANDPA

....
....
....
....

GREAT
GRANDPA

GREAT
GRANDMA

GREAT
GRANDPA

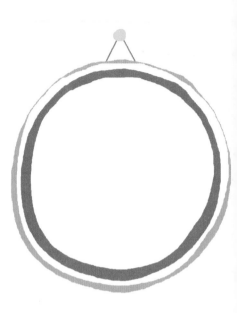

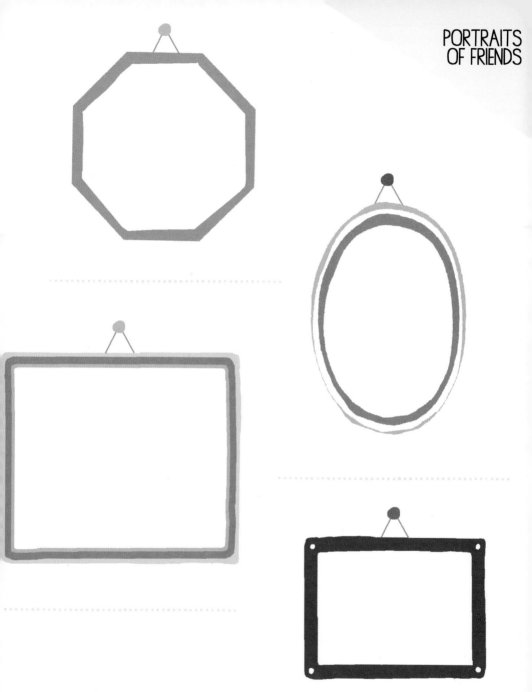

BRILLIANT SCRIBBLE HERE

DATE: ....

MEDIUM: ....

FROM THE COLLECTION OF: ....

SALE PRICE: ....

THINGS YOU'VE ALREADY DECIDED TO DRAW ON:

- ☐ WALL
- ☐ FLOOR
- ☐ BATHTUB
- ☐ MY ARM
- ☐ AN IMPORTANT BANK STATEMENT
- ☐ THE DOG
- ☐ THE FRIDGE
- ☐ THE SOFA CUSHION
- ☐ _____
- ☐ _____

MASTERED
THE ART OF
THE SWADDLE

SLEPT
THROUGH
YOUR FIRST
PARTY

COST OF A
LOAF OF BREAD

WORLD
POPULATION

BUFORD
POP   1
ELEV   8000

WAS A
POPULAR SONG

COST OF A
FIRST-CLASS STAMP

WAS THE MOVIE EVERYONE
WAS TALKING ABOUT

WAS PRESIDENT OF
THE UNITED STATES

COST OF A
GALLON OF GAS

WAS IN THE NEWS

NOTHING BUT A
PUDDLE

ROLLIN'
ROLLIN' ROLLIN'

SITTING UP &
STAYING PUT
(POTTED PLANT MODE)

STARTED ROLLIN':

· ·

SITTING UP:

· ·

CRAWLIN' AROUND:

· ·

FIRST STEPS:

· ·

RUNNIN' THE SHOW:

· ·

OTHER FUNNY THINGS TO NOTE:

· ·

FAVORITE FOODS

- [ ] ....
- [ ] ....
- [ ] ....
- [ ] ....
- [ ] ....
- [ ] ....
- [ ] ....
- [ ] ....
- [ ] ....
- [ ] ....

NOT-SO-FAVORITE FOODS

- [ ] ....
- [ ] ....
- [ ] ....
- [ ] ....
- [ ] ....
- [ ] ....
- [ ] ....
- [ ] ....
- [ ] ....
- [ ] ....

SOFT, PADDED,
GUMMY MILK TEETH

WHO LEFT THE FAUCET ON?

FINALLY, CHIPMUNK
TEETH BREAK THROUGH

BETWEEN SCREAMING, THE
BUNNY STAGE SURE IS CUTE

UH, OH, HERE COME
VAMPIRE FANGS

NOTHING IN THE WORLD
HELPS WITH MOLAR PAIN

- ☐ TUGGING AT EAR

- ☐ CHEWING ANYTHING IN SIGHT

- ☐ SWOLLEN GUMS

- ☐ FLUSHED CHEEKS

- ☐ DROOL MONSTER

- ☐ RESTLESS SLEEP

- ☐ WON'T SLEEP

- ☐ RUNNY POOP

- ☐ DIAPER RASH

- ☐ GRUMPY-MCGRUMPERTON

- ☐ INCONSOLABLE

- ☐ NONE OF THE ABOVE (NOTE: REMEMBER NOT TO GLOAT)

FIRST TIME YOUR EYES FOCUSED ON ME:

FIRST SMILE:

SEEMED REAL

MAY HAVE BEEN GAS

FIRST ANIMAL INTERACTION:

FIRST TIME IN THE OCEAN/LAKE/RIVER:

....

....

....

....

....

FIRST FEVER:

....

....

....

....

....

FIRST TIME YOU WAVED YOUR HAND TO SAY HI:

....

....

....

....

....

weeeoooo
(EACH TIME THE CAR TURNS A CORNER)

(WHEN REALLY TIRED)

noi noi noi

(AS SOON AS YOU SEE FOOD)

thumdumm

FUNNY LITTLE SOUNDS YOU MAKE

- [ ]
- [ ]
- [ ]
- [ ]
- [ ]
- [ ]
- [ ]
- [ ]
- [ ]
- [ ]

WORDS YOU SIGN & SAY

FIRST WORD:

- [ ]
- [ ]
- [ ]
- [ ]
- [ ]
- [ ]
- [ ]
- [ ]
- [ ]

FIRST CRUSH: THE GARBAGE TRUCK

FIRST SOCIAL EVENT:

....

FIRST PARTY:

....

PEOPLE YOU SMILE AT WHILE OUT & ABOUT:

....

FAVORITE PLAYDATES:

....

PEOPLE THAT MAKE YOU EXCITED:

....

FLIRT, SHY, OR EXTROVERT:

....

PASTE PHOTO OR DRAW FAVORITE OUTFIT

WHAT YOU WORE HOME FROM THE HOSPITAL:

MOST IRRESISTIBLE OUTFIT:

FUNNIEST THINGS YOU'VE BEEN DRESSED IN:

I WISH YOU'D NEVER GROW OUT OF:

OUTFIT THAT TURNED
YOU INTO A TINY ELF

HOUSEPLANTS BEWARE

THINGS YOU'VE DESTROYED

- [ ] ....
- [ ] ....
- [ ] ....
- [ ] ....
- [ ] ....
- [ ] ....
- [ ] ....
- [ ] ....
- [ ] ....
- [ ] ....

THINGS YOU'VE TRIED TO PUT IN YOUR MOUTH

- [ ] ....
- [ ] ....
- [ ] ....
- [ ] ....
- [ ] ....
- [ ] ....
- [ ] ....
- [ ] ....
- [ ] ....
- [ ] ....

WHISPER TRAIN

SLEEPING BABIES

ZEN AND THE ART OF SLEEP

ARE YOU ASLEEP YET?

PLEASE FALL ASLEEP

SLEEP FOR SALE

GOOD NIGHT, GOOD NIGHT

FRIENDS FALL ASLEEP

DON'T CRY OVER LACK OF SLEEP

KEEP QUIET BOOK

A DEFINITE THEME IS DEVELOPING

BOOKS WE READ TO YOU

- [ ] ....
- [ ] ....
- [ ] ....
- [ ] ....
- [ ] ....
- [ ] ....
- [ ] ....
- [ ] ....
- [ ] ....
- [ ] ....
- [ ] ....
- [ ] ....

SONGS WE SING TO YOU

- [ ] ....
- [ ] ....
- [ ] ....
- [ ] ....
- [ ] ....
- [ ] ....
- [ ] ....
- [ ] ....
- [ ] ....
- [ ] ....
- [ ] ....
- [ ] ....

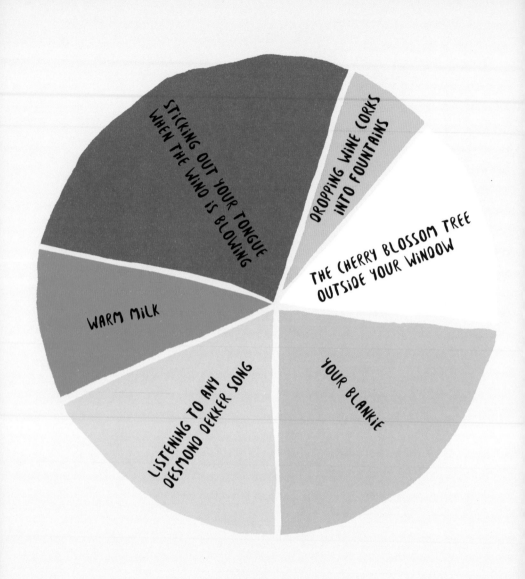

HAPPINESS IS . . .

PERSON TO LAUGH AT: ....

THING TO CUDDLE WITH: ....

TIME OF DAY: ....

TOY TO PLAY WITH: ....

THING TO STARE AT: ....

WAY TO GET AROUND: ....

THING TO DO AT THE PARK: ....

TRICK TO SHOW OFF: ....

CHARACTER TO SEE: ....

PLACE TO TAKE A NAP: ....

FACE TO MAKE: ....

ANIMAL SOUND: ....

UNDER THE RESTAURANT TABLE GUILT

- [ ] TANTRUM AT THE GROCERY STORE

- [ ] DIAPER BLOWOUT AT FAMILY OCCASION

- [ ] FOOD TOSSING IN PUBLIC

- [ ] ....

- [ ] ....

- [ ] ....

- [ ] ....

- [ ] ....

- [ ] ....

- [ ] ....

- [ ] ....

CHARTS, NOTES & INFO, OH MY!

FEEDING CHART

	DATE:	DATE:	DATE:
MORNING 6:			
7:			
8:			
9:			
10:			
11:			
NOON 12:			
1:			
2:			
3:			
4:			
5:			
EVENING 6:			
7:			
8:			
9:			
10:			
11:			
UGHH 12:			
1:			
2:			
3:			
4:			
5:			

POWERED BY MAMA

DATE:	DATE:	DATE:	DATE:

OUNCES / SIDE

FEEDING CHART

	DATE:	DATE:	DATE:
MORNING 6:			
7:			
8:			
9:			
10:			
11:			
NOON 12:			
1:			
2:			
3:			
4:			
5:			
EVENING 6:			
7:			
8:			
9:			
10:			
11:			
UGHH 12:			
1:			
2:			
3:			
4:			
5:			

TINY BUT HUNGRY

DATE:	DATE:	DATE:	DATE:

OUNCES/SIDE

DIAPER CHART

	DATE:	DATE:	DATE:
MORNING 6:			
7:			
8:			
9:			
10:			
11:			
NOON 12:			
1:			
2:			
3:			
4:			
5:			
EVENING 6:			
7:			
8:			
9:			
10:			
11:			
UGHH 12:			
1:			
2:			
3:			
4:			
5:			

LIFE WILL NEVER BE THE SAME

DATE:	DATE:	DATE:	DATE:

WET/DIRTY

DIAPER CHART

	DATE:	DATE:	DATE:
MORNING 6:			
7:			
8:			
9:			
10:			
11:			
NOON 12:			
1:			
2:			
3:			
4:			
5:			
EVENING 6:			
7:			
8:			
9:			
10:			
11:			
UGHH 12:			
1:			
2:			
3:			
4:			
5:			

AGAIN? REALLY?

ATE:	DATE:	DATE:	DATE:

WET/DIRTY

SLEEP
RECORD

	DATE:	DATE:	DATE:
MORNING 6:			
7:			
8:			
9:			
10:			
11:			
NOON 12:			
1:			
2:			
3:			
4:			
5:			
EVENING 6:			
7:			
8:			
9:			
10:			
11:			
UGHH 12:			
1:			
2:			
3:			
4:			
5:			

OPEN 25 HOURS

DATE:	DATE:	DATE:	DATE:

WENT TO SLEEP / WOKE UP

SLEEP RECORD

	DATE:	DATE:	DATE:
MORNING 6:			
7:			
8:			
9:			
10:			
11:			
NOON 12:			
1:			
2:			
3:			
4:			
5:			
EVENING 6:			
7:			
8:			
9:			
10:			
11:			
UGHH 12:			
1:			
2:			
3:			
4:			
5:			

GOOD THING YOU'RE SO CUTE

DATE:	DATE:	DATE:	DATE:

WENT TO SLEEP / WOKE UP

GROWTH
CHART

MY, HOW YOU'VE GROWN

AGE	WEIGHT	HEIGHT
BIRTH		
3 DAYS		
1 WEEK		
2 WEEKS		
3 WEEKS		
1 MONTH		
2 MONTHS		
3 MONTHS		
4 MONTHS		
6 MONTHS		
9 MONTHS		
1 YEAR		

- [ ]
- [ ]
- [ ]
- [ ]
- [ ]
- [ ]
- [ ]
- [ ]
- [ ]
- [ ]
- [ ]

PEDIATRICIAN VISIT: QUESTIONS & NOTES

WE THINK WE ARE:

☐ THE HAPPIEST PARENTS IN THE WORLD

☐ GOING TO CRY ANY SECOND NOW

- [ ]
- [ ]
- [ ]
- [ ]
- [ ]
- [ ]
- [ ]
- [ ]
- [ ]
- [ ]
- [ ]

☐ ....

☐ ....

☐ ....

☐ ....

☐ ....

☐ ....

☐ ....

☐ ....

☐ ....

☐ ....

☐ ....

THINGS WE THINK ABOUT WHILE FEEDING YOU AT 3 A.M.:

☐ WHERE HAVE YOU BEEN ALL OUR LIFE?

☐ SLEEP AS WE KNOW IT IS CLEARLY OVER

- [ ]
- [ ]
- [ ]
- [ ]
- [ ]
- [ ]
- [ ]
- [ ]
- [ ]
- [ ]
- [ ]

WE'RE FINALLY GETTING THE HANG OF:

- [ ] READING YOUR MIND
- [ ] THE MOBY WRAP

☐
☐
☐
☐
☐
☐
☐
☐
☐
☐
☐

PEDIATRICIAN VISIT: QUESTIONS & NOTES

- [ ]
- [ ]
- [ ]
- [ ]
- [ ]
- [ ]
- [ ]
- [ ]
- [ ]
- [ ]
- [ ]

WE'RE NO LONGER:

- [ ] SCARED OF OUR BABY
- [ ] SURE WHERE THAT YEAR WENT

TAKING
STOCK

1 WEEK OLD

PASTE PHOTO OR DRAW

YOU CAN: ....

YOU HAVE: ....

A MOMENT WE DON'T WANT TO FORGET: ....

....

....

....

....

....

....

....

....

....

2 WEEKS OLD

PASTE PHOTO OR DRAW

YOU CAN: . . . .

YOU HAVE: . . . .

A MOMENT WE DON'T WANT TO FORGET: . . . .

1 MONTH OLD

PASTE PHOTO OR DRAW

YOU CAN: . . . .

YOU HAVE: . . . .

A MOMENT WE DON'T WANT TO FORGET: . . . .

. . . .

. . . .

. . . .

. . . .

PASTE PHOTO OR DRAW

YOU CAN: . . . .

YOU HAVE: . . . .

A MOMENT WE DON'T WANT TO FORGET: . . . .

. . . .

. . . .

. . . .

. . . .

. . . .

. . . .

. . . .

. . . .

. . . .

3 MONTHS OLD

PASTE PHOTO OR DRAW

YOU CAN: . . . .

YOU HAVE: . . . .

A MOMENT WE DON'T WANT TO FORGET: . . . .

. . . .

. . . .

. . . .

. . . .

. . . .

. . . .

. . . .

. . . .

. . . .

PASTE PHOTO OR DRAW

YOU CAN: ....

YOU HAVE: ....

A MOMENT WE DON'T WANT TO FORGET: ....

....

....

....

....

....

....

....

....

....

5 MONTHS OLD

PASTE PHOTO OR DRAW

YOU CAN: ....

YOU HAVE: ....

A MOMENT WE DON'T WANT TO FORGET: ....

....

....

....

....

....

....

....

....

....

6 MONTHS OLD

PASTE PHOTO OR DRAW

YOU CAN: . . . .

YOU HAVE: . . . .

A MOMENT WE DON'T WANT TO FORGET: . . . .

. . . .

. . . .

. . . .

. . . .

. . . .

. . . .

. . . .

. . . .

7 MONTHS OLD

PASTE PHOTO OR DRAW

YOU CAN: . . . .

YOU HAVE: . . . .

A MOMENT WE DON'T WANT TO FORGET: . . . .

. . . .

. . . .

. . . .

. . . .

. . . .

. . . .

. . . .

. . . .

8 MONTHS OLD

PASTE PHOTO OR DRAW

YOU CAN: ....

YOU HAVE: ....

A MOMENT WE DON'T WANT TO FORGET: ....

....

....

....

....

....

....

....

....

....

9 MONTHS OLD

PASTE PHOTO OR DRAW

YOU CAN: ....

YOU HAVE: ....

A MOMENT WE DON'T WANT TO FORGET: ....

....

....

....

....

....

....

....

....

10 MONTHS OLD

PASTE PHOTO OR DRAW

YOU CAN: ....

YOU HAVE: ....

A MOMENT WE DON'T WANT TO FORGET: ....

....
....
....
....
....
....
....
....
....

PASTE PHOTO OR DRAW

YOU CAN: ....

YOU HAVE: ....

A MOMENT WE DON'T WANT TO FORGET: ....

....

....

....

....

....

....

....

....

....

1ST
BIRTHDAY

PASTE PHOTO OR DRAW

YOU CAN: ....

YOU HAVE: ....

A MOMENT WE DON'T WANT TO FORGET: ....

....

....

....

....

....

....

....

....